How Animals Behave

ANIMAL DEFENCES

Jeremy Cherfas

CASSELL

Contents

Introduction	3		
Chapter 1 Staying Alive	4	Borrowed weapons	20
Chapter 2 Hide and Seek	6	Chapter 5 Deception	22
Armour	7	Monarchs and viceroys	22
Camouflage	8	Fooling your enemies	24
Disguise	10	Two heads and no tail	26
Chapter 3 Be Alert	12	Chapter 6 Fighting and Defence	27
The selfish herd	13	A useful rule	27
Sentries	14	The last resort	28
'You can't catch me'	15	Close combat	29
An angry mob	16	Astounding Facts	31
Chapter 4 Attack Back	17	Glossary	31
Poisons	18	Index	32
The bombardier beetle	19	Further Reading and Study	32

Note to the Reader

In this book there are some words in the text which are printed in **bold** type. This shows that the word is listed in the Glossary on page 31. The glossary gives a brief explanation of important words which may be new to you.

Cassell Publishers Limited
Villiers House, 41/47 Strand,
London WC2N 5JE, England

Text © Jollands Editions 1991
Illustrations © Cassell Publishers Limited 1991

All rights reserved. No part of this publication may be reproduced or transmitted in any form or by any means, electronic or mechanical including photocopying, recording or any information storage or retrieval system, without prior permission in writing from the publishers.

First published 1991

British Library Cataloguing in Publication Data
Cherfas, Jeremy
  Animal defences. – (How animals behave)
  1. Animals. Self-protection
  I. Title II. Series
  591.57

ISBN 0–304–31972–4

Editorial planning by Jollands Editions
Designed by Alison Anholt-White

Typeset by Fakenham Photosetting Ltd
Colour origination by Golden Cup Printing Co., Ltd,
  Hong Kong
Printed in Great Britain by Eagle Colourbooks Ltd.
  Glasgow

Front Cover: The graceful chameleon puts on a defensive display as an enemy approaches. Chameleons are found in East Africa.
(Photo by Kim Taylor, Bruce Coleman Ltd.)

Back Cover: The author (Photo by Rachel Pearcey)

Introduction

Think of a fox trying to eat a hedgehog, or a cheetah sprinting after a gazelle. The **predator**, the fox or the cheetah, does its best to try and catch its **prey**. At the same time the hedgehog or the gazelle does its best to stop the predator. The hedgehog rolls up into a ball and relies on its needle-sharp spines to put the fox off, while the gazelle twists and turns and tries to tire the cheetah. Either way, the prey is defending itself against the predator, and usually the prey wins. Cheetahs lose the race four out of five times and very few hedgehogs are eaten by foxes.

The prey wins because it has more at stake. The cheetah is only chasing after its dinner, while the gazelle is running for its life. If the cheetah misses, it says hungry a little longer. If the gazelle does not get away, it dies. Gazelles that are not so good at escaping are quickly weeded out.

Most things do not want to be eaten (though we will meet a few that do in the next chapter). So they have defences. They may run, like gazelles, or be protected with spines, like hedgehogs: defence comes in many forms, some of which we explore in this book.

The Australian echidna or spiny anteater has sharp spines as a defence against enemies. This one is burrowing to escape.

A zebra, seen in East Africa, runs for its life with a cheetah in hot pursuit. Gazelles and zebras, though slower than cheetahs, have greater staying power.

1 Staying Alive

Animals must eat to live. Some eat plants, some eat other animals, and some eat both, but all animals need food.

Very few animals gain anything by being eaten, but there are exceptions. **Parasites**, for example, are living things that live and feed on another creature. The fleas that bite my cat and suck her blood are parasites. The cat is their **host**. But there are also parasites that live inside their host, and many that have to spend part of their life in one host and the rest in another. To get from one to the other, some need to be eaten. And to do that, they can change the way the first host behaves.

There is a parasitic worm that spends the first part of its life in a small water animal, a bit like a shrimp, and the rest in a mallard duck. When the parasites are ready to change hosts, they make the shrimp behave oddly. Normally, the shrimp avoids light, and stays near the bottom of the water out of the way of hungry mallards. But when the shrimp is infested with parasites, it swims towards light. That takes it up, to near the surface, where it is much more likely to be eaten by a dabbling duck. So the parasite gets eaten too, and can complete its life cycle inside the duck.

A cat flea as seen greatly magnified amongst the hairs of a cat's fur. Less than two millimetres in length, the flea feeds on the cat's blood. These small parasites are very difficult to dislodge. They jump when disturbed, but cannot fly.

In ancient Greece a parasite was a person who fed beside another person at that person's expense. In biology, a parasite lives on another animal, or inside an animal's body. The diagram shows the life cycle of a parasitic worm that brings about the death of freshwater shrimps and disease for the mallards that eat the shrimps.

This pill woodlouse, photographed in South Africa, has rolled itself into a tight ball as a means of defence. The hard plates which cover the insect's body overlap snugly as it rolls itself up.

Most animals, however, must avoid being eaten. They may have sharp spines. They may disguise themselves, or hide. They may even attack back. You can think of many other kinds of defence. The means of defence vary from one **species** of animal to another, but they all increase the animal's chances of survival. An animal that survives will breed, and its offspring may inherit the defences that kept their parents alive. But other animals have ways to overcome those defences. If they did not, they would not be able to eat or breed.

Freshwater shrimps are to be found in ponds and lakes in most parts of the world. There are many species, but one in particular becomes a host to parasitic worms on the bed of the lake. Bloated with parasites, the shrimps move towards the surface and are gobbled up by mallard ducks.

5

2 Hide and Seek

One of the simplest ways of staying safe is to hide, and many animals defend themselves by hiding. Even an animal as soft and defenceless as an earthworm is well protected within its burrow. The worm digs by making its front end long and thin and poking it between crumbs of soil. Then it grips with special spines and contracts so that it becomes short and fat. That pushes the soil to make good walls for the hole. If the soil is too hard, the worm can eat its way through.

Earthworms come up at night, looking for leaves that they pull down into the burrow to eat. Even then, they leave their tails in the burrow so that they can retreat at the first sign of danger. During the day, they stay safe underground, but at dawn and dusk a bird might catch the worm out of its burrow, and tug until it gets the worm loose.

Many animals that come out at night spend the day in a hole or burrow. One that never comes up is the mole. It spends all its time underground and eats the earthworms that accidentally break through and fall into the mole's tunnels.

A European song thrush tugging at an earthworm caught out of its burrow during daylight hours. The best time for birds to find worms is when a garden is being dug or a field is being ploughed. This is why you can often see a flock of birds behind a tractor as it ploughs a field.

This song thrush is displaying its skill as it cracks open a snail on an anvil. The sound of a bird cracking snails on a stone may help you to find a bird's anvil.

Armour

Even simpler, perhaps, than digging a hole is to cover your body with armour plating. Snails and their relatives are good examples. Snails have one shell, into which they can retreat, while their relatives the **bivalves** have two shells that shut together. Mussels and oysters are bivalves.

Shells are good protection against most predators, but there are some that have found a way through the armour. Thrushes in the garden are good at smashing snails on favourite stones, called anvils. If you look carefully, you might be able to find an anvil, surrounded by broken snail shells.

The thrush and its anvil are proof that no defence is perfect. Whatever protection an animal may come up with, some other animal is going to find a way round it. Life is a constant arms race. If one side comes up with an improvement, such as a tougher shell, the other will come up with an improved method of attack, perhaps by pecking a hole through the shell instead of trying to break it.

Snails are very slow-moving and cannot escape from enemies. The shells carried on their backs give some protection to their soft bodies, but are no defence against hungry birds.

HIDE AND SEEK

Camouflage

Some animals are hard to find even when they are out in the open. They blend into the background, because they look similar to their surroundings. This is called **camouflage**. One of the experts at camouflage is the ptarmigan, a kind of grouse that lives high up on hilltops and moorland.

In summer, you can almost step on a ptarmigan before you see it, so well do its patchy brown feathers hide it in the heather. In winter, when the ground is covered with snow, the same brown feathers would stick out like a sore thumb. So the ptarmigan, like many other animals, changes colour. It becomes almost completely white.

Ptarmigans live in those parts of the world where there is snow during the winter months, in Canada and northern Europe. The plumage of these birds changes colour with the seasons, so that they are well camouflaged throughout the year.

HIDE AND SEEK

A chameleon photographed on a bush in northern Kenya. These animals can lighten or darken their skin in a split second to match the surroundings. Keeping stock still, the chameleon waits for its prey. Then it shoots out its long tongue and traps a passing insect. The chameleon's camouflage is also a means of defence.

The ptarmigan takes a few weeks to moult its brown feathers and grow new white ones. Other animals change much more quickly. You may have heard of the chameleon, which can alter its colour and pattern quickly to match its background, but other animals can do the same trick. Flatfish, like the plaice, match whatever they are resting on, whether it is sand, pebbles, or a checkerboard put there by a scientist.

Camouflage is important for predators too. Lions, for example, hide by stalking quietly through the grass, and also by coming from downwind, so that the breeze does not blow their scent to the prey.

The plaice is an European flatfish that often lies on the sea-bed where it feeds. It reacts to danger by changing colour and pattern to blend in with the different coloured pebbles over which it lies.

HIDE AND SEEK

Disguise

What is the difference between camouflage and disguise? I think it is that a camouflaged animal looks like its surroundings, while a disguised one resembles something else.

Take stick insects, for example. They look exactly like the branches they rest on, and even sway convincingly in the breeze. I think they are disguised, but you may think they are camouflaged. It does not really matter. What matters is that many animals go to extraordinary lengths to look like something they are not.

Insects are experts at this kind of disguise. There are insects that look like leaves, some green and alive, others brown and withered. Some insects look like thorns, and some are exactly like small pebbles or stones. But insects are not the only animals that go in for this kind of deception.

This South American stick insect is difficult to spot in its disguise as a twig. Legs and body have the same slender shape as the twig on which the insect rests.

This leaf insect from the rain forest in Costa Rica is well disguised as a dead leaf. Shaped like a leaf, it even shows blotches and decay marks. Only a very wily bird would recognize this insect as a possible meal.

10

HIDE AND SEEK

The sargassofish lives amongst the sargassum weed that floats on the surface of tropical oceans. It is so like the weed in appearance that it is almost impossible to see. Its disguise, and the weed itself, protect it from attack by larger fish. In the photograph, the eyes of the fish may help you to find it.

Many kinds of fish look like dead leaves and one, which lives in the Caribbean, can even change colour to match the mangrove leaves floating around it in the water. Some snakes are long and thin and green, and you could easily mistake them for a vine growing through the bushes. There is even a frog that looks exactly like a bird dropping. It sits out on a leaf, quite exposed, and predators ignore it.

Usually, a disguise like this works well as a defence. But there is a problem. What if a predator learns to look for things that look like bird droppings? It can become good at telling the real thing from the fakes, and the frogs will not be protected any more. This sort of thing does happen.

When I go looking for mushrooms in the woods, it takes me ages to find the first few. Then, when I have learned to see them hidden among the leaves, I will say, 'I've got my eye in.' From then on, I see mushrooms everywhere. The same applies to a bird searching for hidden food. At first it keeps missing, but once the bird gets its eye in, the food is no longer safe.

3 | Be Alert

One of the best ways to avoid being captured is to be on the look-out. That way, you might see your enemy in time to hide or run away. The problem is, if you spend all your time watching for predators, you don't have the chance to do other vital things, like eating or drinking. To solve this problem, animals come together in groups.

A flock of birds, feeding on the lawn, is like an animal with eyes in the back of its head. While most are feeding, one or two will be looking for danger. If they see something, and fly off, the whole flock will join them and escape. The birds in a flock don't actually take turns; it is just that when there are many birds, one or two are always on the alert. The more birds there are in a flock, the more time each of them can spend feeding, without being in any more danger.

A meerkat watching out for danger. You can read more about these alert little animals on page 14.

Brent geese inhabit the waste lands of northern Asia and North America. Many of them spend the winter in northern Europe. Most of these birds are feeding with heads down. But a few in the flock are on the alert for danger.

The selfish herd

There may be another good reason to be in a group: it confuses predators. Think of a single herring, swimming along. If you were a predator, a tuna perhaps, it would be easy to follow it and swallow it. Now think of a huge school of thousands of herring, each shining with bright flashes of silver as they swim. It is much harder to keep your eye on one particular fish, and when the fish feel threatened they twist and turn even more, making it harder still.

Although a large school may be easier for the predator to find, it makes it harder for the predator to pick off one particular fish. In a large school, each fish has a greater chance of survival. There is safety in numbers.

This large school of fusilier fish, photographed near Fiji in the Pacific Ocean, presents a difficult target for a shark or other predator. Though the school of fish is easily seen, the predator is confused by the size of the school. For the fish, there is safety in numbers.

BE ALERT

Sentries

Flocks of birds and schools of fish do not have proper look-outs; all the animals are alert some of the time. Meerkats are just one of the species where animals take it in turns to perform sentry duty.

Meerkats are small animals, not much bigger than rats, and they live in family groups in southern Africa. Their homes are often dug in abandoned termite nests. When they come up out of their burrows, one or two meerkats will stand on guard. They climb to the top of the termite nests, and often stretch up on their back legs to get a better view.

If the sentry sees something, like an eagle high up in the sky, it gives a sharp alarm call. All the meerkats stop what they are doing and keep their eyes on the eagle. If it flies away, they will go back to what they were doing; feeding, playing, grooming or whatever. But if the eagle shows any signs of wanting to come in for a meal, all the meerkats will dash down into the safety of their burrows.

After a while, the sentries may get tired. Or perhaps they are hungry, or want to join in the games. They make a special noise, and another member of the pack will come and relieve them.

The eagle can probably see that the meerkats have spotted it. Other animals make it quite clear that they have seen the predator.

Meerkats keep watch over their den in Namibia, Africa. These little animals live in groups of twelve or more. Normally, one or two act as look-outs while the others feed or play, but these meerkats are all on the alert because they have spotted the photographer.

BE ALERT

'You can't catch me'

Springbok, like meerkats, also live in southern Africa. They are small antelope, and they are called springbok because they do just that, spring into the air like living pogo-sticks. The animal leaps up, arching its back and putting its head down, a bit like a bucking bronco. This is called pronking or stotting, and many deer and antelope do it.

The sight of a springbok pronking like this is a sure sign that there is a predator, usually a lion or a cheetah, nearby. Pronking not only warns the others in the herd, who often start to pronk themselves, but also sends a message to the predator. It is the springbok's way of telling the predator that it has lost the element of surprise, so it may as well give up and hunt somewhere else.

Two springbok, one of them pronking, in the Kalahari desert, Africa. These small antelopes are on the alert for danger all the time. Pronking is a sign to other springbok that there is a predator nearby. A pronking leap may reach three or more metres in height, and the springbok may pronk five or six times in succession.

An angry mob

Sometimes, it is difficult to tell what exactly is the most important form of defence for a group of animals. Small birds, like chaffinches, gather in large flocks in the winter. The large flock has many eyes on the lookout for danger. That makes it easier for all the birds to escape.

If a hawk does attack, it will be confused by the number of targets. Often, a bird of prey like a hawk will try and split one chaffinch off from the flock, so that it can concentrate its attack.

When they see a hawk, or an owl resting in a tree, the little birds often go on the attack themselves. They form an angry mob, diving at the bigger bird's head and pulling at its feathers. If they keep it up, the bird of prey will tire of this harassment, and flap off in search of a quieter spot. By being alert, confusing, and angry, the chaffinches have successfully defended themselves.

Eagles are recognized by other birds as being dangerous predators. This unusual picture shows an Indian steppe eagle being mobbed by a team of angry but courageous crows.

The marsh hawk or harrier of North America is a bird of prey that usually flies to and fro over a piece of land, harrying it until the prey is found. Here a marsh hawk is being harassed, or 'buzzed', by a single, much smaller red-winged blackbird. Perhaps it has a nest nearby, and wants the marsh hawk to go away.

4 Attack Back

Sometimes it is hard to know when defence ends and attack begins. Many animals have spines to protect themselves, and like the hedgehog and the echidna they may roll up in a ball so that all the predator sees is the spines. The porcupine, which also has spines, turns the tables on any animal foolish enough to attack it.

The porcupine walks backwards towards the predator, shaking and rattling its pointed **quills**. If the animal gives up, well and good. But if it persists, the porcupine rushes back suddenly and sticks its quills into the animal's face. The quills are very loosely attached to the porcupine, and come away, remaining stuck in the predator. They also have small **barbs**, which stop the quill coming out. The wounds made by the quills often become infected, and even animals as big and fierce as tigers have been found dead with hundreds of porcupine quills stuck into them.

An East African crested porcupine displaying its quills. The quills are very sharp and are used as a means of defence. They are controlled by strong muscles in the animal's skin. It is similar muscles that make a cat's fur stand up when it is frightened or angered.

17

ATTACK BACK

Poisons

Sometimes even spines are not enough, and many animals have poisons as well as spines. The scorpion fish, which is named after another poisonous animal, is just one of several species of fish that have sacs of poison at the base of the rays in their fins. If a predator threatens it, the scorpion fish first displays its gaudily coloured fins. This is a warning not to go any further.

If the predator does attack, the scorpion fish manoeuvres to pierce the attacker with its spines. The pain of the poison is intense, and most predators quickly flee. One that does not is the octopus. For reasons nobody understands, the poison has no effect on the octopus. When an octopus approaches, instead of displaying boldly, the scorpion fish turns tail and flees.

Scorpion fish have long, sharp spines which can inflict very painful wounds on an enemy. A number of different species of these fish are found throughout the world.

ATTACK BACK

The scorpion fish does not use its poison spines aggressively, nor to catch its own food. They are only defensive. Quite often, however, poison is used for attack and defence. Venomous snakes, for example, use their poison to kill their food, and usually they escape from predators themselves by silently slithering off. But if there is no escape, they will also use their poison to defend themselves.

The bombardier beetle

Nasty chemicals are a very common defence, and one of the strangest weapons belongs to the bombardier beetle. These beetles are found all over the world, but especially in South America. When they are attacked, usually by ants, they spray a boiling hot liquid from the tip of the **abdomen**. That quickly gets rid of the ants.

The bombardier beetle is like a living chemistry set. In its abdomen it has two compartments, which contain chemicals that are perfectly safe on their own. But when they are mixed, there is a violent chemical reaction that produces heat and gas. The gas blows the boiling mixture out, and the beetle can swivel its abdomen to aim the jet of boiling liquid at whatever has disturbed it.

The bombardier beetle is one of nature's freaks. When threatened by, for example, a frog, it can attack back by spraying a blast of unpleasant liquid from a kind of cannon in its hind quarters. It can swivel this cannon in several directions. The boiling liquid is produced inside the beetle when certain chemicals react with each other. A few squirts of this foul liquid are quite enough to make the frog back off.

ATTACK BACK

A large sea anemone enclosing and stinging a fish called a grouper, in the Coral Sea, Australia. The wavy tentacles are all covered with stinging cells.

Borrowed weapons

Most animals have their own weapons, but a few borrow them from some other species. Some sea-slugs borrow stings, and some caterpillars and butterflies borrow poisons.

Sea-slugs are related to snails, but do not have shells. You might think that would make them defenceless, but it does not. Fish avoid eating sea-slugs, even when the fish are hungry, and the reason is that the sea-slug has stinging cells that can inject the fish with poison. The sea-slug gets its defences by feeding on sea-anemones.

Sea-anemones have wavy tentacles that are covered with stinging cells. They use their stinging cells to capture food and to defend themselves against anything that wants to treat them as food. When anything touches a stinging cell it shoots out a spine that pierces whatever triggered it and injects a poison.

Stinging cells protect the sea-anemone from almost all predators, but not quite all. Sea-slugs somehow manage to eat the tentacles without triggering the stinging cells. Not only that, the stinging cells move through the sea-slug's body to bumps, a bit like tentacles, on its back. There, they protect the sea-slug from predators, just as they protected their former owner, the sea-anemone.

A sea slug, seen at Mauritius, ejecting a number of sticky white strings as a means of defence. The sea slug is poisonous and hungry fish keep away.

ATTACK BACK

Another borrowed weapon is the bad taste of the monarch butterfly. Birds, such as blue jays, like to eat butterflies. The first time a blue jay sees a monarch, it will catch and eat it. But the monarch contains chemicals that make the blue jay quite ill. It may even vomit. From then on, it will not eat monarch butterflies.

Monarchs normally lay their eggs on plants called milkweeds, which contain poisons. Most animals avoid the milkweed, but monarch caterpillars can cope with the poison. In fact, the caterpillar stores the poison. When it has changed into a butterfly the poison eaten by the caterpillar protects the butterfly. If you feed the caterpillar on cabbages, the adult butterflies taste good and blue jays will eat them quite happily.

The beadlet anemone is found in most parts of the world, including Europe and Australia. As shown in the diagram, the tentacles can be folded inwards when the anemone is covered by water or disturbed. One anemone has about 200 tentacles! These are used for catching small animals and for defence against enemies.

5 Deception

Monarchs are protected by the poisons they pick up from milkweeds, but they still have to teach birds to leave them alone. They make it easier for the bird by having a bright pattern that is easy to recognize. This is called warning coloration, and it is very common; animals that are well protected send out a signal that it is best to leave them alone. The skunk, sauntering along in its bright black and white coat, advertises its ability to spray a very nasty smell. The rattlesnake buzzes a warning to prevent you coming closer.

These warnings make sense, because if a predator learns to avoid such animals it runs less risk of being harmed. And the prey, giving out the signal, may avoid being injured itself. But some animals that send out realistic warning signals actually have no protection at all.

Monarchs and viceroys

In the old days of the British Empire, the viceroy stood in for the monarch. The same happens among butterflies. There are butterflies, called viceroys, that look very like monarchs. The differences between them are slight, and certainly enough to fool even a keen-eyed bird. A jay that has tasted monarchs will leave viceroys alone too.

The striped skunk of North America raises its black-and-white tail as a warning. If that fails to stop an enemy, the skunk gives off a very unpleasant smell.

The monarch butterfly (left) is poisonous to birds, but its mimic, the viceroy (right) is not. Both species look very similar. They are found in North America.

This form of defence is called **mimicry**. Of course, the frog we met on page 11 is mimicking a bird dropping, but usually mimicry means copying another animal that has its own protection, rather than merely being disguised.

One mimic that fools many people is the hoverfly, found in many gardens. Hoverflies have black and yellow stripes, and at first glance they look just like bees or wasps. Look closer, and you can see that the eyes, the wings and the head are really quite different. But it is that first glance, when it might be a bee, that protects the hoverfly from hungry birds.

This kind of mimicry is very common. For example, there are harmless snakes with the same colour pattern as poisonous ones. There are grasshoppers that mimic bombardier beetles, and spiders that look like ants. In Borneo, there are five species of tree shrew that taste awful, and five species of squirrel that taste good, but look so like the tree shrews that it takes an expert to tell them apart. In all of these cases, the mimic is harmless, but it copies a species that is not.

A hoverfly collecting nectar from garden mint. At first sight, these flies look very much like bees and wasps with their yellow and black markings. But they have no stings. They are found in many parts of the world.

DECEPTION

Fooling your enemies

The little hog-nosed snake, normally found in North America, is totally harmless. When approached by something large and threatening, it lies perfectly still, relying on its camouflage. But if the threat comes closer the snake begins to writhe and hiss alarmingly. It really is frightening. Every time I have disturbed a hog-nosed snake I have taken a giant leap backwards, scared out of my skin. I am sure other animals do the same, and while the predator is deciding what to do next the little snake slides quietly away and hides.

These two snakes from the rainforest of Costa Rica with their bright warning colours are difficult to tell apart. But the one above is a harmless mimic of the deadly coral snake shown in the lower picture. The safest way for any animal is to avoid both of them.

DECEPTION

Seen in the grasslands of Africa, this plover is defending its nest site from an approaching warthog. The plover limps away from the nest and pretends to be injured by flapping one wing. After a time the warthog will lose interest and go away.

Birds do not often have complicated defences because usually they can simply fly away. But what about young chicks, who cannot yet escape? Quite often they are well camouflaged, and at the first sign of danger they freeze, making it very hard to spot them. Even that, however, may not be enough, and so in some species the parent bird goes through an elaborate bit of acting.

When a fox comes close to a ringed plover hidden on her nest, she will sneak quietly away from the eggs or chicks. Then she pops up and attracts the fox's attention. She walks away from the nest, crying piteously and fluttering one wing and dragging it on the ground. The fox certainly seems fooled by all this, because he stalks off after her. But when she has led him away from the nest she leaps up into the air, her 'broken' wing miraculously healed, and flies back to her young. She settles down quickly, relying on her camouflage to protect her until another fox comes too close.

Two heads and no tail

While plovers distract their predators by pretending they are injured, skinks pretend that they have two heads. Skinks are lizards that live in Australia, but unlike most lizards they have very short, stumpy tails. In fact, their tails look very like their heads, and that is their defence. Predators have a hard time deciding which end to attack. If they peck at the tail, the skink has a chance to run down its burrow.

Some lizards go even further in their attempts to distract a predator. They shed their tails completely. The tail is designed to break off, and carries on twitching and wriggling for a while even though it is no longer attached to the lizard. While the predator is deceived by this strange distraction, the lizard runs off. In time it will grow a new long tail.

Skinks are Australian lizards. The blue-tongued skink (above) has a sturdy tail similar in size and shape to its head and shoulders. The stump-tailed skink (below) has a short, stubby tail which looks very much like its head, particularly when curled in defence, as in the picture.

6 Fighting and Defence

Most of this book is about the ways in which animals defend themselves from predators who want to eat them. The predator and its prey are almost always different species of animal. There is another kind of defence, though, the kind an animal might use when it fights with one of its own species. It could be a dispute about food, or about a **territory**, or about mating. But these fights are not because one animal wants to eat the other.

In any fight there is a good chance that the loser may be severely wounded or even killed. But the winner may be injured too, and unable to defend itself against a predator. So it pays the animals to settle their dispute without actually fighting, if at all possible. That is their best defence.

A useful rule

One of the simplest ways to settle a dispute over ownership is to obey a rule, such as 'finders keepers'. Some animals obey that particular rule. The speckled wood butterfly lives in English woodlands, and in spring the males occupy territories. These territories are the patches of sunlight that filter down through the leaves on to the forest floor. The male sits there, waiting for a female to arrive, and when one does, they fly up into the leaves to mate.

A male and female fox having an argument. Ears back, jaws open wide, and the crouching position are all signs of aggression in an animal. This sort of behaviour seldom turns into a real fight.

The speckled wood butterfly is found in English woodlands. This picture shows a female (left), and male (right). The male likes to establish his territory in patches of sunlight below trees.

27

FIGHTING AND DEFENCE

Sometimes, however, it is not a female but another male who lands in the patch of sunlight. When that happens, the two males fly spiralling up into the treetop. One flies off, the other returns to the patch. The odd thing is, it is always the one who was there first who remains. It does not matter how big the intruder is, or how fast he flies, or anything. He always loses. The finder of a patch always keeps it.

In fact, the dispute between the two speckled wood butterflies is hardly a fight at all. It seems instead to be a mistake, quickly sorted out. The resident stays and the intruder retreats because they both obey the same rule. The only time there is anything approaching a real battle is when two males settle at each end of a particularly large patch of sunlight. Each thinks he is the resident, and when they do finally meet, each expects the other one to retreat. These fluttering fights can last several minutes.

The last resort

Not all animals obey rules as simple as the speckled wood butterfly's, but for most of them an actual fight is usually the last resort. They have all sorts of ways of protecting themselves against the damage of a fight. In general, you could say that before they decide to fight, they size up their opponent very carefully.

Brown bears wrestle with each other in the icy waters of Alaska, USA.

Two male red kangaroos fighting. One of these Australian animals will soon give in. Neither of them can afford to be injured.

FIGHTING AND DEFENCE

Sometimes there is a fight between two rival stags. With their antlers locked, they push and shove in head-to-head combat. The winner of the fight becomes master of the herd.

Red deer stags are a perfect example. In the mating season, called the rut, each stag tries to keep control over a group of **hinds**. He roars out across the glens to advertise his presence. Another stag, who might be thinking of challenging the owner for his hinds, will begin by roaring too. The owner, hearing this, will roar back.

Stags have to put a great deal of effort into roaring, so the stronger a stag is, the faster he can roar. That is the first clue. If the owner can roar more often, he is probably stronger and would win a fight. The challenger's best defence is not to attack.

Close combat

If their roaring is similar, the animals may come closer together. They walk up and down, next to one another. Each is checking the other one out, seeing how big he is, how large his antlers are, and whether he is in fighting trim. Again, the challenger will proceed only if he thinks he stands a good chance of winning. If he withdraws, the owner lets him go.

The antlers of the red deer stag are a sign of his power and strength. At the beginning of the mating season rival males bellow and roar at each other across the Scottish highlands. This is called belling.

FIGHTING AND DEFENCE

Very occasionally, the challenger decides to risk a fight. The stags rush at one another, and the mountains echo to the crashing of their antlers. Now the fight is for real, and each tries to do as much damage as possible while protecting himself. They push and shove and try to trip each other. The sharp tines of the antlers stab and wound. Eventually, one animal is defeated and staggers off. The winner may enjoy his ownership of the females for a while, but another challenge is sure to come.

Stags do everything they can to avoid a real fight, and that is true of most animals. Very few attack without reason, only when they are hungry or feel threatened themselves.

In this book we have explored many of the defences animals use against predators in order to avoid being eaten. But it is different when it comes to a fight with a member of the same species; the best defence then is to avoid a fight unless you have a good chance of winning.

Timber wolves testing each other's strength in the Canadian forest. This sort of play seldom turns into a real fight.

Astounding Facts

- The pancake tortoise of Africa has a soft shell, not much good as armour plating. But when the tortoise is threatened, it crawls into a crack between two rocks and puffs itself up, wedging itself tightly in place.
- The date mussel dissolves a protective burrow in limestone by producing an acid that eats away the rock.
- There is a Japanese crab whose back looks exactly like the face of an angry Samurai warrior. Although it is good to eat, the local fishermen are superstitious and never eat it. When they catch one they always throw it back. This might be the reason why this species has survived.
- A caterpillar from Borneo fastens flower buds to its body to disguise itself. When the buds wilt, the caterpillar replaces them with fresh-cut flowers.
- Some moths send out an **ultrasonic** signal of their own when they hear a bat hunting nearby. It may jam the bat's sonar, or it may be a warning that the moth tastes bad.
- An electric eel, weighing 40 kilograms, can deliver a shock of 650 volts, enough to kill a person touching it.

Glossary

abdomen: the hind part of an insect's body. In mammals, the abdomen is the belly.

barb: a backward-pointing spine that stops a hook, or harpoon, or arrow, or quill from being pulled out.

bivalve: an animal with a shell made of two halves. They are hinged so that the shell can open or close. Mussels and clams are bivalves.

camouflage: patterns and colours that help an animal to blend into its background.

hind: female deer.

host: a plant or animal that gives food and protection to a parasite.

mimicry: imitating another species.

parasite: a small animal or plant living inside or on the surface of another one.

predator: any animal that hunts and eats other animals. Lions are predators.

prey: animals that are hunted and eaten as food by other animals.

quill: a long, hollow rod, like the central rod of a feather, or the spine of a hedgehog or porcupine.

species: a class of animals or plants that look alike. Members of one species cannot usually breed with those of another species.

territory: an area of land in which an animal or group of animals live. Animals mark out and protect their territories.

ultrasonic: describes a sound so high-pitched that it cannot be heard by the human ear.

Index

You can use this index for looking up different animals, and the parts of the world where some of them are found. Where a page number is printed in *italic* (slanting) type, it means that there is a picture of that animal on that page, as well as text.

Africa 14, 15, 25
Alaska 28
anemone *20*, *21*
antelope 15
ants 19, 23
Asia 12
Australia 3, 20, 21, 26, 28

beadlet anemone *21*
bee 23
blackbird *16*
blue jay *21*
blue-tongued skink *26*
bombardier beetle *19*, 23
Borneo 23
brent geese *12*
brown bear 28

Canada 8, 29
Caribbean 11
chaffinch 16
chameleon 9
cheetah *3*
Coral Sea 20
coral snake 24
Costa Rica 10, 24
crested porcupine *17*
crow *16*

deer 15, *29*, *30*

eagle 14, *16*
earthworm 6

East Africa 3, 17
echidna *3*
England 27
Europe 3, 6, 8, 9, 12, 21

Fiji 13
flea *4*
freshwater shrimp *4*, *5*
frog 11, 19, 23
fusilier fish *13*

gazelle 3
grasshopper 23
Greece 4
grouper *20*

harrier *16*
hawk *16*
hedgehog 3, 17
herring 13
hog-nosed snake 24
hoverfly 23

India 16

jay 21, 22

Kalahari desert 15
kangaroo 28
Kenya 9

leaf insect *10*
lion 9
lizards 26

mallard *4*
marsh hawk *16*
Mauritius 20
meerkat *12*, *14*
mole 6
monarch butterfly 21, *22*
mussel 7

Namibia 14
North America 12, 16, 22, 24

octopus 18
owl 16
oyster 7

parasite worm *4*
pill woodlouse *5*
plaice 9
plover *25*, 26
porcupine *17*
ptarmigan 8, 9

red deer *29*, *30*
red kangaroo 28
red-winged blackbird *16*
ringed plover 25

sargassofish *11*
scorpion fish *18*
Scotland 29
sea anemone 20
sea slug *20*
shrimp *4*, *5*

skink *26*
skunk *22*
snail 7, 20
snake 24
South America 10, 19, 24
speckled wood butterfly *27*, *28*
spider 23
spiny anteater *3*
springbok *15*
squirrel 23
steppe eagle *16*
stick insect *10*
stump-tailed skink *26*

termite 14
thrush 6, 7
tiger 17
timber wolf *29*
tree shrew 23
tuna 13

viceroy butterfly *22*

warthog *25*
wasp 23
wolf *29*

zebra 3

Further Reading and Study

If you have enjoyed reading this book and want to learn more about animals and how they behave, there are several things you can do:

- You can read the other five titles in this series. They are listed on the back cover. This will widen your knowledge of animal behaviour.

- Learn all you can about the animals that interest you most. Look them up in a natural history encyclopedia or other reference book.

- Learn about other series of books dealing with wildlife, for example:
  Discovering Nature series published by Wayland
  Eyewitness Guides published by Dorling Kindersley, and by Collins in Australia
  Mysteries and Marvels of Nature published by Usborne
  Today's World published by Watts/Gloucester

- If you have a pet, increase your knowledge of animal behaviour by watching how your pet behaves.

Picture Acknowledgements

The publishers wish to thank the following photographers and agencies whose photographs appear in this book. The photographs are credited below by page number and position on the page, B bottom, T top, L left, R right:

Bruce Coleman Ltd: C. B. & D. W. Frith 3T, Kim Taylor 4T, 6, 7T, G. Doré 7B, Wayne Lankinen 8T, Bernd Thies 8B, Jane Burton 9T, M. P. L. Fogden 10B, 24T, 24B, Jen and Des Bartlett 11, 18, Rod Williams 12T, Carl Roessler 13, 20T, Gunter Ziesler 14, Jill Sneesby 15, Joseph Van Wormer 17, Bob and Clara Colhoun 22T, Nevill Coleman 26B, George McCarthy 29B, Hans Reinhard 30, Dennis Green 27B. Frank Lane Picture Agency Ltd: Silvestris 3B, Leonard Lee 10T, W. S. Clark 16T, Frank Lane 20B, L. West 22 (both), Philip Perry 25, David Grewcock 27T, W. Wisniewski 28B, Terry Whittaker 29T, Mark Newman 16B, 28T. Eric and David Hosking: D. P. Wilson 9B. Nature Photographers Ltd: S. C. Bisserot 5B, 26T, Paul Sterry 5T, 23, Roger Tidman 12B, James Hyett 21.